"Parents who share this book with their children will be helping their children face some of the problems of growing up and, at the same time, will show their children that these are problems that can be solved together."

—Gary Bodner, Ph.D.,
Director of the Adolescent Treatment Program, Charter Pacific Hospital, Torrance, CA

"This book is a superb tool for parents and educators to use in helping children to understand their emotions."

—National Kid Watch Program
(1-800-KID WATCH)

SOMETIMES IT'S O.K. TO BE ANGRY!

Praise for books in the *It's O.K.* series

"An extremely useful book that give lots of practical advice to parents. The most useful and charming part of the book is a series of stories which parents can read to and then discuss with their children. The lessons are, we think, acceptable, unfrightening and effective because they are presented in this dialogue form. We strongly recommend this book."

—Mrs. Louise Bates Ames,
Associate Director, Gesell Institute
of Human Development, author of
syndicated newspaper column, "Parents Ask"

"The authors help parents and children to communicate openly, building trust. This is the best book of its kind I've seen. The authors know kids and know how to address them, soundly, compassionately, and entertainingly."

—*Chicago Tribune*

SOMETIMES IT'S O.K. TO BE ANGRY!

A PARENT/CHILD MANUAL FOR THE EDUCATION OF CHILDREN

Dr. Mitch Golant with Bob Crane

Illustrated by Frank C. Smith

AN RGA PRODUCTION

TOR

A TOM DOHERTY ASSOCIATES BOOK

Books in the It's O.K. series

IT'S O.K. TO BE SHY!
IT'S O.K. TO SAY NO!
IT'S O.K. TO SAY NO TO DRUGS!
SOMETIMES IT'S O.K. TO BE ANGRY!
SOMETIMES IT'S O.K. TO TELL SECRETS!

SOMETIMES IT'S O.K. TO BE ANGRY!

Copyright © 1987 by RGA Publishing Group, Inc.

First printing: October 1987

A TOR Book

Published by Tom Doherty Associates, Inc.
49 West 24 Street
New York, N.Y. 10010

Cover art by Frank C. Smith

ISBN: 0-812-59460-6
CAN. ED.: 0-812-59461-4

Printed in the United States of America

0 9 8 7 6 5 4 3 2

SOMETIMES IT'S O.K. TO BE ANGRY!

A PARENT/CHILD MANUAL FOR THE EDUCATION OF CHILDREN

Introduction

Anger is a complex emotion. We are often frightened by our anger when we let it out in destructive ways. On the other hand, we can also feel the effects of holding in our anger—an upset stomach, high blood pressure, or headaches.

Finding a proper balance and expressing our anger constructively are important but difficult emotional tasks. We are not born with an instinctive knowledge of how to focus anger properly and use it for our benefit. That is something that must be learned.

Your willingness to talk with your child about his or her feelings and experiences can redirect his or her manner of expressing anger. Children don't have to express anger in a destructive manner. They also don't have to suppress it and turn their anger inward.

The purpose of this book is to guide you in helping your child to channel his or her anger in constructive ways.

Chapter One

How can I teach my child that it's O.K. to be angry?

To feel anger is neither good nor bad. It is a normal and legitimate reaction to feeling wronged, whether that wrong is real or imagined.

It is what we do with our anger, how we act when we are angry, that is important. For example, when we lash out in anger, later we may feel worse in remorse. However, when we discuss our hurt with someone who is understanding, we may feel better. And talking with the person who caused the hurt in the first place may create a stronger bond between you and that person.

It is difficult for children to make the distinction between the emotion of anger and what is done with that anger. To a child, they are one and the same. Nevertheless, a child needs to learn the difference between the two.

If we are to separate the two in the child's mind, we parents must communicate the difference. We can teach a child that he or she can feel angry and express that anger, yet not be destructive. In other words, it is O.K. to be angry, but it is not O.K. to behave in a destructive manner out of anger.

It is very important to make this distinction with your child. He or she should not be chastised for feeling angry, only for destructive behavior. Eventually the child will learn the difference between feeling angry and acting out that anger in harmful ways.

If your child expresses his or her anger destructively, try to respond helpfully, saying, "You are entitled to be angry. That's O.K. But I don't want you to hit anyone," or "I don't want you to damage anything, including yourself."

Children have a difficult time communicating their emotional reactions because they lack the language needed to translate what they feel into words. Parents should help their children to express verbally what they feel when they are angry. You know your child best. Look for subtle clues of unexpressed anger. Two of the most common signs are pouting or sulking and an "I don't care about anything" attitude. But each child will have his or her own signals.

Remember, admitting that he or she feels angry is difficult for a child to do. It will take some time and practice before your child feels comfortable expressing anger verbally. You may have to ask your child a series of questions about why he or she is angry.

Tommy and Billy, both four years old, were playing with toy trucks. Soon Tommy's mother heard them fighting. She separated the boys, then sat down to talk to them.

MOTHER: Tommy, you hit Billy and you know you're not supposed to do that. I can understand your being angry. That's O.K. But it's not O.K. to hit. Tell me what upset you.

TOMMY: Billy took my truck. It's mine and he can't have it.

MOTHER: O.K., I see why you were upset, but it's still not good to hit someone. You should have told Billy how you felt, instead of hitting him.

TOMMY: He won't listen, no matter what I say.

MOTHER: How do you know, if you don't even try? And if he didn't, you could have come to me for help.

TOMMY: I guess so.

11

MOTHER: So if Billy makes you angry like that again, you speak up
and tell him that you're angry and that you don't want him to do
that again. If he doesn't listen to you, then come to me. It's
O.K. to be angry, but you are not allowed to hit anyone or do
anything destructive. Do you understand?

Another approach Tommy's mother might use to encourage an
appropriate reaction to anger would be to remind him of a time when
he made her angry. She could remind Tommy that she talked with him
about her feelings and didn't hit him.

Before we attempt to teach our children to deal properly with their
anger, we need to look at ourselves and evaluate the ways we cope
with anger. Our behavior serves as a model for our children's actions.
Children are great imitators. Ask yourself what your child may be
learning about expressing anger from the way you deal with a difficult
situation.

Let's look at an example of a parent's anger, in a situation where
that anger is caused by the child's actions.

Terry is eight and loves his collection of toy cars. He prefers to play with his cars in the bathroom, because he likes the noise they make when he runs them across the tiled floor.

Terry is careless about picking up his cars from the bathroom floor. His mother has warned him that leaving them there could be very dangerous if someone were to step on them.

One day Terry's mother went into the bathroom in her bare feet and narrowly missed stepping on one of the cars. Her first reaction, in the heat of anger, was to break the toy. Loss of the car would be a lesson to Terry.

Every parent has this experience at least once, and it is often difficult to resist the destructive urge. It is no easier for a child.

Terry's mother stopped just as she was about to crush the toy. She asked herself, "What kind of message would I send to Terry by breaking his toy?" Terry would be in tears, and his mother would regret her action.

Terry might learn a powerful lesson about leaving his toys where they weren't supposed to be, but his mother recognized that, more important, Terry would get the message that since his mother responded destructively to her anger, perhaps it wasn't all that bad for him to do the same. She couldn't very well expect Terry to "Do as I say, not as I do." Explaining that children and adults don't have to follow the same rules often creates strong resentment in children and makes them see adults as hypocrites.

Instead of breaking the car, Terry's mother picked up the toy, confronted him with the evidence of his misdeed, and told him that, as a consequence, she was going to keep the toy away from him for one week. Terry protested loudly, but he got the message.

An important thing for parents to remember is that their behavior in such situations must be as consistent as possible. The parent must deal with each incident in the same way, and both parents must react appropriately, if they expect their child to learn and understand. And remember to assure the child that you still love him or her, despite the anger.

Chapter Two

What is the proper way to express feelings of anger?

Whether a person is six years old or sixty, anger surfaces in very much the same way. It can rise quickly or burn at a steady rate. It can put someone on an emotional roller coaster. But the expression of anger, we hope, changes as we mature.

The ability to rationalize anger and respond to it constructively is not a natural ability. It takes thought, effort, and will. Any adult can probably think of a time when anger caused him or her to behave almost as a child would, without thought, letting the emotion rule.

The following story illustrates a classic anger-inducing situation. It is included here specifically to show the steps that we adults need to take in order to handle our anger maturely.

Betty has worked four years in the consumer loan department of a branch office of a major bank. She has done an exceptionally good job. Her boss has recognized the quality of her work. In fact, he has promised her a promotion to vice-president at the first opportunity.

One day Betty hears from other workers at the bank that a woman will be brought in from another branch to serve as vice-president.

There are a number of ways Betty might respond to this situation.

She might react by letting her anger take control of her emotions. She might storm into her boss's office and demand confirmation or

denial of the news. If the story is confirmed, and Betty's anger is still in control of her, she might quit on the spot without waiting for an explanation. Though quitting might feel like the right action at the time, Betty would undoubtedly regret the decision.

Another typical reaction would be for Betty to feel shocked and disappointed, then turn her anger inward and become depressed. Betty says nothing of her feelings to anyone, not even her boss. The boss knows he will have to explain to Betty eventually, but if he sees no reaction from her, he will assume that she isn't particularly disturbed by the change in plans, and may feel that his actions were justified. Another result of suppressing her anger is that the resentment Betty feels will almost certainly affect her overall work habits, reducing her chances for promotion.

A third possible reaction: Betty consciously channels her anger. She plans her strategy. She approaches her boss for an explanation. She doesn't let anger get control of her, but uses it in a constructive manner.

I QUIT!

Here is the way the conversation between Betty and her boss might go:

BETTY: I've heard that someone from another branch is coming in as vice-president. You've been promising that position to me. I want you to know that I am very angry, and I feel I deserve an explanation.

BOSS: Betty, I'm sorry to say that the story is true. The news leaked out before I had a chance to discuss the situation with you.

BETTY: Why is this happening? You must realize that this is not only a great disappointment for me, it's an embarrassment as well. The people I work with knew I was in line for that position.

BOSS: Betty, the decision was made over my head at corporate headquarters. They've decided on a major reorganization of consumer loan operations, and if you can be patient, you'll get that promotion anyway, in just a few months. Corporate headquarters knows what a good job you've done. A lot of changes are in the works. I can only counsel you to be patient for a while longer.

Now Betty is not only in control of the situation, she's also gotten her boss to reaffirm his appreciation of her value. If Betty asks for a raise as compensation, her boss would be hard-pressed to resist. In addition, her actions—holding her expression of anger in check, calmly discussing the situation—impress her boss, who notes a mature, dependable worker.

Let's look at those three reactions again. In the first, where Betty lets her anger take control, everyone loses. If Betty follows through on her threat to quit, she's out of a job, and the bank has lost a valuable employee.

Even if Betty's boss talks her out of her threat, she has put him in an awkward position, and he will never entirely forget that. If I promote her, he may think, will she be able to succeed at the job? There are so many pressures; she might explode again, and that would reflect badly on me for recommending her.

In the second reaction, Betty suppresses her anger and says nothing. Her anger will turn into quiet resentment—of her boss, of the bank hierarchy, of the new vice-president, and of herself for her inability to speak up in her own behalf.

Betty may never again be able to do her job without being distracted by the resentments created by her anger. The job she once loved may become a chore.

In the third solution, Betty consciously channeled her anger and used it to her advantage.

Consider how her direct communication of anger affected her relationship with her boss: Having promised Betty a promotion and having

been temporarily overruled by a decision of the bank's administration, her boss found himself in a difficult position. He hesitated to break the news because he didn't want to lose Betty. By communicating in a clear manner, Betty made her feelings known and gave her boss an opportunity to respond appropriately. They had a dialogue and everyone came out ahead.

Now let's look at some children in anger-causing situations.

Donnie is seven and the one thing he wants more than anything else is a bike. His parents know it. They've been considering buying him one, but have one major concern. The family's home is on a very busy thoroughfare, and Donnie's parents are concerned for their son's safety. In addition, some of the older boys in the neighborhood are occasionally reckless in their bike riding, and Donnie's parents fear that he will emulate them.

Donnie's parents decide against buying him a bike, and tell him of that decision. Donnie can react in a number of different ways.

He might storm about the house, slamming doors and shouting. That reaction would earn Donnie a reprimand. And it would also confirm his parents' decision by demonstrating that he is still too immature to take on the responsibilities of a bike.

Or Donnie might react by suppressing his anger, saying little and sulking. His anger might show in little ways, such as forgetting to do his chores or neglecting his schoolwork. His parents would resent such an attitude.

Donnie's anger might surface in some mildly destructive way. The boy may do something his parents don't like and blame his actions on the fact that they haven't given him a bike. This simmering resentment may be even more unbearable for the parents than an explosive reaction would be. Pouting is a punishment, a childish method of retaliating against someone who caused hurt. It masks feelings of angry alienation.

What would be a more constructive approach? You cannot expect most children to act anything other than their age. It is the parents' responsibility to teach and enlighten. Donnie's parents need to sit down with him and explain their position, how their primary concern

is for his safety. They should encourage him to express his feelings about their decision. The conversation might be something like this:

FATHER: Donnie, you know your mom and I love you very much. We know that you want a bike very badly, but we've decided that it's better to wait a little while before giving you one.

DONNIE: But why, Dad? It's not fair. You promised.

MOTHER: Donnie, I understand your being angry. But the street here is terribly busy and we've noticed that some of the older boys in the neighborhood ride their bikes recklessly. We're afraid that you might be influenced by them.

DONNIE: It really isn't fair. I know the street is dangerous. I wouldn't ride my bike there. I'd walk it around the corner to the side streets where it's safe. And I'd never do some of the things those older kids do. They're crazy. I don't pay any attention to them. Honest, I'd be very careful with a bike. You wouldn't have to worry about me.

FATHER: Well, if we saw you riding a bike on the street here or imitating those older boys, we'd take away your bike privileges for a few weeks. How would you feel about that?

DONNIE: Well, I guess I'd understand.

FATHER: Donnie, suppose we make a deal. We'll talk about this again one month from today, and reconsider the decision. How's that?

DONNIE: A whole month? Well . . . O.K., I guess.

22

The conversation has given Donnie an opportunity to express his anger, and a reasonable compromise has been worked out. Donnie's parents have helped him to understand their concerns for his safety. And Donnie has gained his parents' concession to reconsider their decision in a month.

This and similar experiences will teach Donnie that the conscious channeling of anger into constructive communication can prove beneficial to him.

Remember, too, that children notice their parents' interaction. When you and your spouse are involved in an argument, your behavior will convey a lot to your child. Children of violent or sulking and resentful parents cannot be expected to learn to express their own anger in beneficial ways. Children learn not only from lecture but from observation.

Chapter Three

How can I teach my child to channel anger properly?

The key to teaching is communication. You need to communicate clearly to your child, and you need to encourage your child to explain and discuss his or her feelings when angry.

Let's look at some examples. Bobby is four and has a new baby sister, Rachel. Bobby resents the attention being paid to his baby sister, and he makes no effort to hide that resentment.

One day Bobby's mother finds him leaning over the baby's crib, poking at her. Her natural reaction might be to chastise Bobby severely, but that will not constructively respond to his anger. It would only exaggerate the feelings of alienation and resentment that have caused his misbehavior.

His mother takes Bobby aside and speaks to him about his behavior. "Bobby, I know you feel hurt and angry because we're paying so much attention to your little sister. When you were a baby, we gave you a lot of attention, just as we are now with Rachel. We still love you very much, but Rachel is very little right now and can't do anything for herself, so she needs extra care. But that doesn't mean that we love you any less. We love you as much as always. Now, tell me what makes you angry toward Rachel."

Bobby is likely to say something like: "I hate her. I don't want her around." Or, "You don't love me as much as before."

A loving approach is needed. Bobby's mother can say, "Bobby, I love you and I understand how you feel. I felt the same way when my younger brother was born. It's natural for you to feel that way. But I won't let you hurt Rachel, and I know you really don't want to hurt her. Whenever you feel angry toward Rachel, come tell me about it. It's O.K. to feel angry, but it's not O.K. to do anything that might hurt her. And if you think we're not paying enough attention to you, all you have to do is say so."

It might be helpful if his mother gave Bobby a doll on which to act out his feelings. If Bobby can direct his anger toward the doll and communicate his feelings in a safe, supportive environment, he will learn that by expressing his anger in a constructive way he can release his hostility and still feel good about himself. His parents must make sure that he knows that anger is perfectly permissible; what is not permissible is the destructive expression of that anger.

Destructive behavior is a cry for attention. Bobby's anger and resentment toward his little sister arise from his concern that he is losing parental love. If he is permitted to express his feelings in play or with his parents, and is reassured that his parents love him as much as they always have, Bobby is not as likely to focus his anger on his baby sister. Bobby needs to have permission to feel the way he does with the support of unconditional love from his parents. Such reassurances are positive reinforcement for his positive communications about his anger.

Molly is nine. One day while Molly was taking a test at school, her teacher found some notes on the floor next to her desk. He immediately assumed that Molly was using the notes to cheat on her test. He reported Molly to the principal, who notified her parents. Molly had protested her innocence, but neither the teacher nor the principal believed her.

Molly was upset about the incident, but she was also angry that her father had not believed her. When her father talked to her that evening, he was torn between his faith in Molly and the statements of the teacher and the principal.

First he urged Molly to tell her side of the story and to express her

feelings about the incident. Molly explained what had happened, and protested that the notes were not hers and that she hadn't even seen them until the teacher found them.

Her dad said, "Molly, I believe you are telling me the truth. How do you feel about this?"

Molly said, "It's so unfair, Dad. I've never cheated in school, and my teacher and the principal treated me like some kind of criminal just because those papers were near my desk."

Her dad said, "Since you've been wrongly accused, you have every right to feel angry. I think the two of us should go and talk with the principal and your teacher, and you can tell them exactly how you feel."

Molly said, "Do I have to, Dad? They scare me, and I don't think they'll believe me anyway. Adults never believe kids."

Her father said, "Molly, that's not true, and it's certainly not the point. If you feel you've been treated unfairly by someone, you have a right to tell them how you feel. You're angry about it. And when you hold that anger inside, it comes out in other ways, ways that could lead to problems. You have to talk to the people who've made you feel angry."

Molly and her father met with the principal and her teacher the next day at school. Molly told her accusers that the notes weren't hers, and her father supported her. After some urging from her father, Molly told the teacher and principal how she felt about being unfairly accused. They were not convinced of her innocence, though she spoke clearly and did not shout.

Molly's dad said, "If Molly had been cheating, wouldn't the answers from the notes be on her test paper? Why don't you compare the two?"

They did. Molly had missed two questions that she would have gotten right if she had been using the notes. The principal and the teacher apologized, and the teacher also promised to apologize to Molly in front of the class, which taught Molly another lesson about facing up to your mistakes in a mature fashion.

On their way home, her father asked Molly how she felt about the incident.

"I feel much better, Dad," she said. "I know I was right, but I was afraid that no one else would know that."

Her father said, "Don't ever be afraid to speak up for yourself when you feel you've been wronged. And remember that when you express your anger maturely instead of acting like a baby, the people you're angry with are much more likely to listen to you."

When a child feels wronged, it is important that he speak up for himself. While that may not resolve the problem immediately, it is likely to dissipate his anger.

A parent or any other "authority figure" who refuses to listen to a child's viewpoint about any real or imagined hurt only ends up encouraging the child to turn his or her feelings off. Listening, even if you don't agree, is all you have to do. In turn, this also helps the child to respond to other people who may be angry at him or her. Approaching situations in this manner teaches children that other opinions are valid and provides valuable training for social interaction outside the home.

Sometimes, no matter how much encouragement you give him, it is not possible for a child to confront the source of his anger simply because he has not developed the emotional or intellectual skills necessary to locate it. For situations such as those, you can encourage your child to display his anger to you. Let him act out his feelings, with you as the focus.

This has two potential benefits for the child: First, it will alleviate the stress that has been building up, because all of us—young or old—feel better when we convey our feelings of anger to someone, even if that person is not the cause of our anger. A sympathetic listener can provide a healing, therapeutic experience.

Second, under the guiding hand of a loving parent who has the child's best interests in mind, the child can practice focusing his or her anger in an appropriate manner. With the parent acting as a sort of therapist, the child will learn how to express his or her anger without being destructive.

Janie is on her grammar school's girl's swim team. Her coach is a strict disciplinarian and won't listen to what she deems "back talk" from her team. Janie has real potential as a swimmer, and

the coach wants to motivate her, so she often rides her very hard in practice.

Janie only vaguely understands why the coach treats her the way she does. Although she has an inkling that the coach thinks she's special, Janie still feels that she is unnecessarily mean to her. Sometimes she hates the coach because of the way she acts.

Janie's mother understands her anger. She encourages Janie to talk about swim practice and her relationship with the coach. With her mother as a substitute for the coach, whom Janie doesn't feel comfortable confronting directly, Janie openly and freely discloses her feelings of anger.

These encounters help Janie to maintain her composure during arduous practice sessions. She knows that no matter how angry she may get at the coach, she will have the opportunity to vent that anger when she gets home. The process has become a game to her, and during practice she can visualize the exchange that will take place later, making it easier to cope with the situation.

Janie's mother does not allow inappropriate behavior during the role-playing sessions, and Janie has learned to show anger in a manner that can be understood and appreciated by the person at whom it is directed. Janie is acquiring skills that will benefit her all her life.

Richard is seven and occasionally reacts badly if he doesn't get his way when playing with friends. Sometimes he'll throw or break toys. If, for example, he is playing a board game with a friend and is losing badly, he may shout and toss the game to the floor.

Richard's parents have scolded him when they have seen him behave this way, but it doesn't seem to affect his behavior.

Richard has to learn to put his feelings into words. That will take time, and requires patience on his parents' part. Instead of scolding him after an outburst of temper, Richard's parents need to take him aside and discuss his actions calmly. They should urge Richard to explain why he reacted as he did. The conversation might sound like this:

PARENT: Why did you behave that way, Richard?

RICHARD: I was mad.

PARENT: Because you were not winning the game.

RICHARD: Yeah. I like to win. But I was making stupid mistakes. That's why I was losing.

PARENT: It sounds as though you were angry at yourself.

RICHARD: I guess I was.

PARENT: Well, Richard, we all make mistakes. Fifteen minutes ago, I was calling your grandmother, and I dialed Mrs. Morrison's number instead. I made a mistake. That's pretty dumb, but things like that happen all the time to everyone. That's normal. You're not a bad person and you're not stupid if you make mistakes. Try to remember that. If you keep behaving like that, your friends might not want to play with you anymore.

RICHARD: Sometimes they ask me if I'm going to get mad before we start to play.

PARENT: Are you interested in knowing what sorts of things you can do when you get angry? [It is important to note that children like Richard who respond to anger destructively often do so because they think they have no other alternatives open to them. Richard's parents need to teach him not only that he has a choice but what some of those choices are.]

RICHARD: O.K.

PARENT: Let's see if any of these ideas help you to feel better. If they don't, we'll try some others. One thing you might try is to pay attention to when you first start feeling angry. Think about what it is that starts you feeling angry. If you're with your friends and you are getting angry with yourself, you might say out loud, "I'm getting frustrated with myself."

For most of us, adult or child, this simple act of evaluating anger and our response to it will create an opportunity to direct it appropriately. Anger and the response to anger seem to be automatically linked, but they are not. Between the onset of anger and our ultimate response is a series of steps. All of these steps put together become greater than the sum of the parts, and we become enraged. The phenomenon takes place in a matter of moments, yet is a distinct chain reaction.

Where we react explosively to anger, there is a next-to-last step in the process where we choose how our anger will manifest. The choice in this case is, "I am going to explode." Anger builds up to the point where the mental pressure gauge almost cannot avoid blowing to let off steam.

By stepping away from ourselves and acknowledging our anger, we give ourselves the opportunity to consider choices other than exploding. Sometimes we blow up anyway, because it is a quick release of tension. But most of the time this is not an appropriate response.

It is important that a commitment be made to seek a less violent option. If we want that commitment from a child, we have to make him or her understand that continued destructive behavior will affect his or her life: Friends will not want to play with him or her, the child's parents will punish him or her. We must also be sure to establish rewards for good behavior—parental praise, additional demonstrations of affection.

Parents must make sure, however, that their children are not merely substituting one bad behavior for another. Watch for signs like sullenness, moodiness, and an uncaring attitude, any of which may suggest that there are feelings that have been left unexpressed.

Chapter Four

What are some other choices for the expression of anger?

There are many alternatives. Here are just a few constructive possibilities:

- Draw an angry picture. Suggest that your child sit down with crayon and paper and draw a picture of her anger. Encourage her to be creative, to show her anger in any form. If she needs some guidance, suggest that she draw a picture of herself and the way she feels, or a picture of the source of her anger, or what she feels like doing out of anger.

- Roar like a lion. This might be startling to you if you are unaware that the child is angry about something, but it's better than destructive behavior.

- Write a letter that is never sent. Encourage your child to sit down and write a letter to whomever he is angry with. Let him write anything he wants. This approach has the added benefit of associating verbal expression with anger. Don't ask to see the child's letter; *you* may be the source of his anger. However, if the child volunteers his letter to you, praise him for putting his anger into words.

If a child uses bad language when angered, urge the child to sit down with some paper and pencil anytime he is angry and write down all the bad words he might want to use. When he is finished, suggest that he crumple up the paper and throw it away in the trash. Again, do not ask to see the list.

- Pound on pillows. The child can vent her anger by pounding on a pillow or other resilient inanimate object. Urge her to go at it really vigorously. This may shorten the life span of whatever you choose for the exercise, but the practice has therapeutic value for venting angry feelings.

- Run and play hard. Suggest that your child release anger by using physical exercise as an outlet. Almost anything that requires a great deal of effort will do the trick, such as running all out or throwing a ball against a wall as hard as possible (and then chasing it). Or you could urge the child to go outside and try to push the house over.

The point of all this is to attempt to find something that enables the child to dissipate his or her anger. If one choice doesn't seem to work, you can suggest another.

There are times when a child will say something hurtful to you while learning to handle anger constructively. Remember that children and adults all say things in anger that they really don't mean. Tell your child that you feel hurt. The child will learn that just as another's words can affect him, his words can affect another.

Later, when everyone's nerves are less inflamed, ask your child if his words were an accurate expression of his feelings. Discuss the situation openly and honestly. That sort of interaction will encourage him to vent his anger (and other feelings) positively in the future.

Chapter Five

On the following pages, you will find a series of stories about children and their reactions to anger-inducing situations. These stories are intended to be read aloud by you and your child.

The purpose of the stories is to help make your child aware that feeling angry is an appropriate reaction to feeling wronged, but that there are right ways and wrong ways to exhibit anger.

These stories illustrate a variety of reactions to anger. While your child may express anger destructively or may suppress it, it is important that you not restrict your reading to stories of similar behavior. Let your child hear both sides.

One of the purposes of these stories is to stimulate discussion between parent and child. Ask your child questions at the conclusion of some of the stories. How does your child feel about the children in the stories and their reactions? Does he or she ever feel like the child in the story? Has he or she ever acted like the child in the story? You can help further discussion by talking about how you expressed anger when you were a child, or how you deal with feeling wronged.

Keep in mind that it isn't necessary to read all the stories at one sitting. Continue reading only as long as your child seems attentive and interested. When his or her interest begins to wane, put the rest of the stories aside for another time.

RANDY'S STORY

   Randy came home from school one day and found his six-year-old brother, Teddy, playing with one of Randy's model airplanes. Randy was eight and was very proud of his model planes. To him, they were the most important things in the world.

   When Randy saw Teddy was playing with his plane, he got very angry. He chased Teddy out of his room, down the stairs, and into the living room.

When he caught Teddy, he started hitting him.

Their mom broke up the fight. "What's going on here?" she said. "Randy, why are you hitting your brother? You know I don't permit that."

Randy told his mom what had happened. She said, "Teddy, you know you're supposed to stay out of Randy's room, and you're also forbidden to touch Randy's airplanes. You were wrong to go in there."

"I'm sorry," Teddy said.

Then their mom turned to Randy. "Young man," she said, "when you are angry at Teddy or at anyone, you are supposed to tell someone what you

are angry about. Being destructive or abusive doesn't help. Now, tell Teddy exactly why you were angry with him."

Randy tearfully explained to Teddy how much work he had put into the model planes and how precious they were to him. And he explained how sad he would be if one of his planes were damaged. Randy felt a lot better after he said all that. Teddy apologized again for what he had done, and Randy said he was sorry for hurting Teddy. They were brothers and friends again.

Hitting somebody doesn't make you feel better. In fact, it usually makes you feel worse because you get angry at yourself. If you were very angry, like Randy, what would you do?

MARCIE'S STORY

Marcie was nine and she loved
books. She was always taking books out of the
library. Once she lent a library book to her friend
Patricia. A week later, she asked Patricia for the
book so she could take it back to the library.

Patricia said she had lost it. "It doesn't matter," Patricia added. "The library can get another one."

Marcie was very upset, but she didn't say anything. She knew she was responsible for the book, and she would have to pay for it. She was angry at Patricia for being careless.

She told her mom what had happened. Her mom said, "Oh, Marcie, Patricia really let you down. I don't understand how she could have lost that book. Did you tell her how you felt?"

"No, Mom, I didn't. I guess I didn't want to hurt her feelings," Marcie said.

"This has nothing to do with Patricia's feelings,

Marcie. She was careless with someone else's property, but you're the person who has to pay for it. You have every right to be angry. You also have every right to tell Patricia that you are angry. You shouldn't let the anger stay inside of you. Tell Patricia what it will cost you to replace that book. I'll talk to her mom about Patricia's bad attitude about other people's property. Maybe they will help pay for the book."

"O.K., Mom," Marcie said, "I'll talk to Patricia. I guess if I lose her as a friend, it won't be much of a loss."

If a friend lost something that belonged to you, how would you feel? What would you do?

JASON'S STORY

Jason was eleven and he had gone to see a great new movie that all the kids were excited about. When he came home, he was very upset.

"Why are people so rude?" he asked his mom as he walked in the door.

His mom said, "What's wrong, Jason? You're home early from the movie."

"I couldn't get in because of four rude kids," Jason said.

"What happened?" his mom asked.

Jason said, "I was waiting in line, and four kids sneaked in up front. The movie sold out when there was just one person ahead of me. I was so angry at those kids."

His mom said, "Jason, if you were so angry about those kids sneaking in line, why didn't you say something?"

"Oh, I don't know, Mom," Jason said. "I guess I just didn't want to make a big scene."

"Well," his mom said, "you could have just said,

'Hey, there's a line here!' I'm sure the other people in line would have supported you completely. They probably didn't speak up for the same reason you didn't. They didn't want to make a scene. That's how rude people keep getting away with being rude."

Jason said, "You know, Mom, you're right. I should have said something. Next time I will."

What would you have done?

HEATHER'S STORY

Heather was eleven years old and very proud of
the fact that she was the regular baby-sitter for
three families in her neighborhood. She liked the kids
and she really liked earning her own spending
money. There was one thing she didn't like, though.
Whenever she went to sit for the Browns, Mrs.
Brown always left a list of other things for her to do,
like putting clothes away or washing dishes. She
always did the jobs, but was angry about it.

One day Heather decided to tell her dad about the
problem. They sat down together in the family
room.

"There's something bothering me, Dad, and I don't
know what to do about it," Heather said. "Whenever
I go to baby-sit for Mrs. Brown, she expects me to do
chores around the house, and she never pays me
for doing them."

"Well," said Heather's dad, "have you ever asked
her to pay you?"

"No," Heather replied, "but she's never offered to,
either, and I think that's what makes me so angry."

"Well, dear, it sounds like you're going to have to
do something about it. Why don't you write down
the different things she asks you to do and then
figure out what each one is worth. Then, the next
time you go to the Browns', you can say that you've

gotten so good at doing those chores you think you ought to be paid for them."

"Sounds like a good idea to me," said Heather, "but what if she stops using me at all? I really like sitting for Julie and Chris, and some money is better than no money."

"Heather, this is one of those times when you have a tough choice to make. You have to decide for yourself what you are going to do, but I think Mrs. Brown is wrong and I think you should stand up for yourself," said Heather's dad.

"You're right, Dad," said Heather. "Even if she does drop me, at least I'll stop feeling angry about the whole thing."

What would you do if you were Heather?

SEAN'S STORY

Sean is on a Little League baseball team. The coach was showing the boys how to bunt, and most of them had lined up to watch, including Sean.

Suddenly, a baseball hit Sean in the back of the head. It didn't hurt, but Sean got very angry. Freddie, Sean's friend, came over to pick up the ball. Sean said very angrily, "Did you throw that ball?"

Freddie said yes. Before he had a chance to say anything else, Sean hit Freddie and knocked him down. The two of them started fighting. The coach came running over to break it up.

"Now, what's going on here?" the coach asked.

Sean said, "Freddie hit me in the head with a baseball, so I hit him back."

Freddie said, "I didn't do it on purpose. The ball slipped out of my hand."

The coach said, "Sean, why didn't you give Freddie a chance to apologize? It was just an accident. You

two guys are friends. You wouldn't deliberately hurt one another, would you?"

Heads bowed, the two of them looked down at the ground and said, "No, sir."

Sean said, "I'm sorry. When I get angry like that, sometimes I do things without thinking."

"Well, Sean," the coach said, "you should *think* when you're angry—you should stop for a moment,

and think about what you're going to do. If you feel as though you want to hit someone, think of something else to do instead. That way you won't hurt someone—or yourself."

"I'll try," Sean said. He apologized to Freddie, and Freddie apologized to Sean.

"I hope there are no bad feelings between the two of you," the coach said.

"No hard feelings?" Sean asked Freddie.

"No hard feelings, buddy," said Freddie, and the two friends got back to practice.

What would you have done if you were Sean? What would you have done if you were Freddie?

GERALDINE'S STORY

Geraldine was playing basketball
in her backyard one day with her friend Virginia.
Geraldine and Virginia were ten and they loved
playing basketball. They both thought they were
just as good at it as the boys their age.

Virginia tried a crazy shot at the basket. The ball
missed completely and bounced over the fence into
the yard of a neighbor, Mrs. Rooney, who was out
working on her flower beds.

Mrs. Rooney got angry when the basketball bounced
into her yard. "Can't you girls keep this ball in your
own yard?" she yelled. Then she picked up the ball
and took it into her house.

Geraldine and Virginia were shocked. Geraldine
went inside and told her mom what had happened.

Her mom said, "Oh, Geraldine, that isn't right at all. Did you tell Mrs. Rooney how you feel?"

"No," said Geraldine, "I was so angry and she was so angry there didn't seem to be anything to say."

Just then the phone rang. It was Mrs. Rooney, asking to speak to Geraldine. When Geraldine got on the phone, Mrs. Rooney said, "Geraldine, I'm very sorry that I got so angry. Sometimes when I get angry I react without thinking, and that's a dumb thing to do."

"I'm sorry about the ball, Mrs. Rooney," said Geraldine, "but we really do try to be careful. It was an accident."

"I know it was an accident—that's why I feel so bad about what I did. Why don't you come over and I'll give you back your ball. Can you forgive me for behaving so badly?"

"It's O.K., Mrs. Rooney. I'll come get the ball right now!"

Geraldine and Virginia both went to Mrs. Rooney's. The girls said they were sorry about the ball going into her yard and Mrs. Rooney apologized again for taking the ball. She gave it back, and Geraldine and Virginia resumed their game. Geraldine was glad that she and Mrs. Rooney had talked.

Sometimes adults react to feelings of anger just as kids do—without thinking. If you were Geraldine, how would you have dealt with Mrs. Rooney's anger?

PETER'S STORY

Peter was nine years old and loved anything that had to do with space. He read everything he could about astronauts and rockets and he was sure that one day he would fly his own ship to the moon.

Every afternoon for a whole week Peter went running into the kitchen saying, "Anything for me, Mom? Did anything come in the mail for me?" and his mom would say, "No, Peter, nothing today."

Finally, one day when Peter came home, there was a box sitting on the kitchen table. "Holy cow," thought Peter. "It's finally here."

"Mom!" he yelled. "Mom—come see what I got!"

"Is this what you've been waiting for all this time, Peter?" asked his mom as she came into the kitchen. "It's got to be something pretty great for you to be so excited."

"It is, Mom. See, I saw this ad in the back of a magazine at the library. This is a working rocket, Mom. It's supposed to be all shiny and it goes eighty

feet up into the air! It cost me plenty but it's worth it if it's as good as it looked in the picture."

His mom said, "Here, Peter, let me cut that last string for you so we can see this wonderful rocket of yours."

The string was cut, and with a huge smile on his face Peter lifted out his new rocket. In an instant the smile was gone and Peter was trying very hard not to cry.

"I guess it doesn't look much like the picture in the magazine, does it, sweetheart?"

"It doesn't even come close, Mom!" Peter yelled. "Look at this—this stupid rubber band is supposed to send it up eighty feet? Hah! I bet it won't even get off the stupid ground!"

"Now, Peter. Calm down. I know you're angry and upset, but there's something to be learned from all this."

"What's that, Mom?" said Peter dejectedly.

"First, you've got to realize that the ad was misleading. It made you believe that the rocket was something it obviously is not. But don't feel bad about believing it. What I mean is, don't be angry at yourself. Be angry at the company who sold it to you."

"I do feel dumb for ordering it. But I am very angry at that company! What can I do?"

"Why don't you write the company a letter? Tell them that the ad made you think the product was something it isn't. And ask for a refund."

"That's a good idea, Mom. Will you help me write it?"

"Sure. And next time you want something you see advertised, come talk to me about it before you spend the money."

What would you do?

AUDREY'S STORY

Audrey was seven and in the first grade. One morning, she went into her room to get her homework and found her little brother Andy sitting on her bed, tearing the pages apart.

She got very angry. She ran into Andy's room and got his favorite coloring book. Then she ran back to her own room and ripped up the coloring book while Andy watched.

Crying, Andy ran downstairs to their mom. Audrey followed. Her mom said, "Audrey, your brother Andy told me that you tore up his coloring book. Why did you do that?"

Audrey told her about Andy tearing up her homework. "I was just getting even with him, Mom."

Her mom said, "Well, I understand that you would be angry with Andy. That was a terrible thing for him to do. It's O.K. to be angry, but why did you behave so destructively?"

"I was trying to teach him a lesson, Mom. I keep telling him to stay out of my room, but he goes in anyway," Audrey said.

"Audrey, if Andy ever does something like this again, you come to me and I'll deal with your brother," Audrey's mom said. "Being angry is O.K., but being destructive out of anger is not."

"I'm sorry, Mom," said Audrey. "I won't do it again. But what am I going to do about my homework?"

Her mom said, "Don't worry, Audrey. Let's see if we can tape it together, and I'll write a note to your teacher."

What would you do if you had a little brother like Andy?

JEFF'S STORY

Jeff had a bad day at school. He came home, slammed the kitchen door, and flung his knapsack down on the table. When his mom asked him what was wrong, he said, "Nothing."

A little later, while he was practicing basketball shots, his brother came out to play with him.

"Why do you always have to be around when I want to be alone?" Jeff yelled. "Just get lost, you little creep." Jeff's brother was very hurt and ran back into the house without a word.

Jeff's mom heard the yelling and came out to see what was wrong. "Why were you yelling at your brother, Jeffrey? You've been in a foul mood since you got home and I'd like to know what's wrong."

Jeff said, "Mom, I don't know what's wrong with me. I feel bad about yelling at Jimmy. But

sometimes I just feel like I have to yell at somebody."

Jeff's mom said, "Honey, everyone gets in a bad mood now and then. But just because you feel like the sun's not shining on you today doesn't mean that you have to make it rain on everybody else. Do you understand?"

"I guess I understand," said Jeffrey. "But I still wish I knew what made me feel this way."

"Jeffrey," said his mom, "there's an old saying about feeling the way you do today. People say you woke up on the wrong side of the bed. It happens to lots of people once in a while. You've just got to try to shake it when it happens to you."

"How do I do that when I feel so angry and mad inside, Mom?" asked Jeffrey.

"There are a few things you can try, Jeffrey. Sometimes when I wake up in a bad mood I just concentrate on trying to smile all day long. Pretty soon I don't have to try anymore. Or sometimes I sing a song to myself."

"I'll try, Mom. Maybe I should go and apologize to Jimmy," Jeffrey said.

"I think that's a good idea. And Jeffrey, next time you're in a bad mood, why don't you tell me? Maybe together we can get you out of it."

There's nothing wrong with being in a bad mood except that you can't really feel happy. What would you do if you woke up in a bad mood?

AMY'S STORY

Amy was ten years old. She did well enough in school—not great, but not too bad, either. She had a few friends, but none were really special, except for Mrs. Haines.

Old Mrs. Haines had lived down the block from Amy for as long as Amy could remember. And for as long as Amy could remember, Old Mrs. Haines had been very, very old. When Mrs. Haines was sick once, Amy's mom had given her some food to take over. Amy hadn't really wanted to go, but once she and Mrs. Haines started talking, it was hard for her to leave. Now they visited almost every day.

"Do you know what, Mom?" Amy said one afternoon. "I think Mrs. Haines is the neatest person in the whole wide world."

"I know you're very fond of her, Amy. She is a very special lady. I like her, too."

One night Mrs. Haines passed away in her sleep. When Amy's mom heard the news the next day,

she called Amy's school and told them she would be right over to pick up Amy.

"Hi, Mom. What's up?" asked Amy as she got into the car.

"Darling, I have some sad news to tell you. Slide over here next to me. Mrs. Haines passed away last night in her sleep. It didn't hurt her. Amy, she had a rich, long life and we should feel happy for her."

"She's dead?" Amy whispered. "How could she die, Mom? She was my best friend!" Amy jumped out of the car and started running down the street.

Amy's mom caught up to her at the park near the school. Amy was sitting on a bench, crying. Amy's mom sat down and put her arms around Amy. She said, "Talk to me, Amy. Tell me what you feel."

"I feel terrible, Mom. I know I should be glad she died peacefully and I know she was ready to die.

She used to tell me she was ready, that she'd lived long enough. But I'm mad at her. I'm really mad. It's just not fair. We had so much fun together and now she's left me."

"Amy, darling," said her mom, "don't think of it that way. She didn't leave you. I'm sure that if she had a choice she would have been your best friend forever. But she didn't have a choice, did she?"

"No, she didn't."

"You have a choice, Amy. You can stay angry and let that feeling spoil your memories, or you can remember and treasure the wonderful times you had with her."

"I don't want to be angry anymore, Mom. I remember all the fun we had. I don't think I'll ever forget her."

"No, sweetheart, I don't think you ever will. You know, you were a very lucky girl to have Mrs. Haines as your special friend. You should feel happy to have known her as long as you did."

"I do, Mom. I'm still sad, but I'm really not angry anymore. Thanks for helping me understand. I love you."

It's O.K. to feel angry when someone you love dies, but staying angry is not O.K. You need to talk to somebody to help you get rid of the anger and keep the good memories.

RUSTY'S STORY

Rusty was nine and he was good in school, especially in math. He could do calculations better and faster than anyone else in his class.

One day in class, Rusty's teacher scolded Bernard, another boy in the class, for not doing his math homework. Rusty knew Bernard had a lot of trouble with math. He liked Bernard, although they really weren't good friends.

After class, Rusty offered to help Bernard with his math work. He said, "I'm pretty good at it, and I'll help you if you want. Maybe you could help me with something later on."

Bernard agreed, and they met for an hour or so after school at Rusty's home. Rusty helped Bernard

a lot. There were a few things that Bernard didn't understand, but when Rusty explained them, they became clear to Bernard. After a few days of Rusty's help, Bernard's math work improved enough that the teacher noticed.

Bernard never said thank you for the help Rusty had given him, and Rusty was upset and hurt by this. Rusty's dad noticed that something was bothering him, and asked about it.

When Rusty explained his anger, his dad said, "Well, Rusty, some people are like that. They forget to thank people for doing nice things for them. Why don't you say something to Bernard? You're not doing yourself any good by stewing over it."

Rusty said, "But what can I say, Dad? I don't want to sound silly."

His dad said, "Well, Rusty, why don't you just say, 'Hey, Bernard, do I get a thank-you for helping you

with your math, or don't I?' You don't have to say it angrily. You could make it sound like a little joke. He'll get the point, I'm sure. When someone does something that makes you angry, you should speak up. And you don't have to make it sound like a challenge."

Rusty did exactly as his dad suggested. Not only did he get a thank-you from Bernard, but he received an apology as well. The two of them became better friends.

What would you do if you helped someone who didn't say thank you?

HARRIET'S STORY

Harriet's mom and dad gave her a little dog for her
ninth birthday. It was a light brown puppy with white
paws that looked like boots. So Harriet named the
dog Boots.

Harriet had wanted a dog for a long time, and she
promised her mom and dad that if she got one, she
would take care of it all by herself. Her dad reminded
her on her birthday that Boots was entirely her
responsibility. That was O.K. with Harriet.

Boots wasn't housebroken, so Harriet found out
from a friend whose dad was a veterinarian how to
teach him. Boots didn't learn very quickly, and after
three weeks of Harriet's best efforts, he still wasn't
housebroken.

One day, Boots made a mess in the living room.
When Harriet saw it, she chased after him with his
leash in hand, and hit Boots very, very hard with it.

Her mom stopped her. She said, "Harriet, I know that you are angry, but I won't permit you to behave that way."

"Oh, Mom," Harriet said, "I'm so angry with that dog! He's so stupid!"

"It's O.K. to be angry," her mom said, "but you're being cruel and you're not helping the situation. If Boots misbehaves again, I want you to think of some other way to vent your anger."

"Like what, Mom?" Harriet asked.

Her mom said, "Pound the pillows on the couch, or dash around the block like mad, or run out in the

yard and yell your head off. Do anything to get the feelings out of your system. You cannot strike the dog, Harriet."

"You're right, Mom," Harriet said. "I know I hurt Boots and I'm feeling bad about it already. I'll be ready to try something else in case he does it again. But I hope he learns soon."

Harriet had to learn that you can't teach a pet anything by hurting it. You've got to love it even more. That goes for people, too. Nasty names or punches and slaps just don't fix anything.

What would you do if you had a problem like Harriet's?

AARON'S STORY

"Hi, Aaron," Aaron's dad said. He'd been out most of the day that Saturday, shopping and running errands. Aaron didn't say hello, just mumbled something. About an hour later, his dad noticed that Aaron was still sulking.

His dad said, "Aaron, you're behaving very strangely. Is something wrong?"

Aaron said, "No, everything's O.K., Dad." But the way he said it told his dad that something was wrong, after all.

"Now, Aaron, I know you better than that," his dad said. "Tell me what's bothering you."

Finally, Aaron blurted out, "You promised to drive me to the movies today."

"Oh, Aaron," his dad said, snapping his fingers, "I

forgot that today was your movie day. I'm very
sorry."

Aaron said, "It's O.K., Dad, I know you're busy and
all that."

His dad said, "Aaron, why didn't you tell me about
this when I first came home, instead of sulking?
You have every right to be angry with me. It was
thoughtless of me to forget."

"I can't be angry with you," Aaron said. "You're my dad."

"Well, Aaron," his dad said, "anytime someone does something wrong to you, no matter who it is, you have every right to get angry, and every right to speak up and tell that person what your feelings are. It would have been better for both of us if you had. If I ever make you angry again, tell me how you feel right away."

"O.K., Dad, I will," Aaron said.

"Good. Is that movie still playing tomorrow?"

"It sure is!" Aaron said, smiling.

"Great! We'll go, and this time I'll even spring for popcorn!"

Aaron and his dad both laughed and felt better.

What do you do when your parents make you angry?

JULIE'S STORY

Julie was nine and a Girl Scout. It was her first year, and she loved everything about scouting—the meetings, the camping trips, the arts and crafts, and all her new friends.

At a meeting one afternoon the troop leaders announced that they had assigned everyone to small groups. Each group of five girls was to create a mural showing what the Girl Scouts meant to them. Julie immediately got what she thought was a great idea—the mural would show the mountains and some tents in the distance, and up close would be lots of girls doing different things.

"I've got a great idea," Julie announced when her group settled down together. She told them what she wanted to do. "It'll be great. I'll do the mountains. Barbie, you can do the tents, O.K.?"

"Wait a minute," said another girl in the group. "I don't think that's such a great idea, Julie. None of us can draw people real well and I want this mural to

be the best. What do you all think about doing a field of pretty flowers and then in little circles around the edge we can draw pictures of some of our badges?"

"Yeah!" said the rest of the girls, and one of them said, "I like to draw flowers, and our badges are so pretty!"

Julie didn't say a word. She kept to herself by the corner of the paper, and when the meeting was over she left without even saying good-bye.

When she arrived home, she was so obviously unhappy her mom said, "Julie, what's wrong? You're usually so bright and happy after your Girl Scout meeting."

"I'm so angry, Mom. We were supposed to do these murals today and I came up with a great idea but nobody listened to me. It really made me mad."

"Did you ask the girls why they didn't like your idea?"

"They said it was because there were too many people to draw and they can't draw people well."

"What was their idea?"

"We ended up doing a field of flowers with pictures of our Girl Scout badges all around. It did look sort of pretty, I guess."

"Julie, it sounds to me like you wanted to put yourself in charge. But in a group nobody's in charge. Everybody works together. That's what makes it so much fun, don't you think?"

"I guess so, Mom. I think I probably was a little bossy, but I was so excited at first . . ."

"Well, Julie, you've got to learn that other people have ideas and opinions, too, and that they want to share their thoughts just as much as you do. I'm not saying you should keep quiet, but maybe you could present your ideas in a different way."

"I'll try, Mom," Julie said.

Suppose you had an idea that nobody else was interested in. Would you get angry, as Julie did?

ARTHUR'S STORY

Arthur was in big trouble with his mom and dad. His dad gave him a stern look and said, "Arthur, you've been accused of cutting down the flowers in front of Mr. Collier's house this morning. What do you have to say for yourself?"

Arthur said, "Who told you that?"

His dad replied, "Never mind who told me. Answer my question."

Arthur knew he was caught. He shrugged his shoulders and admitted that he had cut down the flowers. "I was very angry with Mr. Collier, and I did it to get even with him. Every time we try to play

stickball in the street near his house, he calls the
police to chase us. It really isn't fair."

His dad said, "So you decided out of anger that
you were going to get even by cutting his flowers.
Arthur, as punishment for this action, you are going
to replace those flowers with your own money, and
you are going to plant them, too."

"Aw, Dad," Arthur said. "I was sorry I did it, and
now you're making it worse."

His dad said, "Arthur, I can understand your being

angry about Mr. Collier's actions, but you have to find less destructive ways to express your feelings. The best thing to do when someone makes you angry is to talk to that person about how you feel. Now, I know it's almost impossible to talk to Mr. Collier, so if he makes you angry, try telling me about it. You can get all your feelings out to me. Believe me, I'll understand."

"Okay, Dad," Arthur said, "I promise I will. Now, can we replace those flowers and get this over with?"

If you were Arthur, what would you do?

CLAIRE'S STORY

Claire, who was nine, loved to draw and paint. After school she would sometimes sit and draw for hours, right up to the time her mom and dad called her to dinner. She was always neat and careful with her paints and paper.

One day Claire's dad called to her from the living room. When she got downstairs, she saw that her watercolor tray had fallen off the table and spilled all over the carpeting. Her dad scolded her very harshly for it. Claire tried to tell him what she thought must have happened, but he didn't listen, just yelled and sent her to her room.

Claire was very upset. She went up to her room and closed the door. A little later, her mom came up to talk to her. She could see that Claire was very upset.

Claire told her mom about the watercolor tray. "I think Sam must have knocked it off the table, Mom.

I was going to clean it, but Sam was barking to come in so I put it down for a minute to open the door for him. Then I must have forgotten about it. But Dad didn't even listen when I told him I hadn't been painting in the living room. It's not fair that he yelled at me like that."

Her mom said, "Why don't you tell your dad how you feel?"

Claire said, "Oh, it's no use. He's already made up his mind that I did it."

Her mom said, "Well, Claire, just because we're your parents doesn't mean that we're right all the time. And it doesn't mean that you don't have a right to speak up for yourself. If you are angry, you should say how you feel, no matter who is involved. Why don't you go downstairs and tell your dad exactly how you feel?"

Claire did. After she told her dad what she thought had happened, he apologized for thinking that she was to blame. That made Claire feel much better. She and her dad hugged and made up. When they sat down to dinner a few minutes later, the two of them were smiling and laughing, glad not to be angry anymore.

Sometimes when we do things we know are wrong, we have to accept the consequences. But if anyone assumes that we did wrong when we didn't, then we need to speak up. Would you stay angry at your dad or would you try to talk to him?

MACK'S STORY

Mack, everyone said, was the perfect example of a happy-go-lucky kid. Mack never lost his temper, never let himself feel bad about something for too long, never, in fact, was anything except happy-go-lucky Mack. He was a good friend to a lot of people and many looked upon him as a big brother, someone who could help them with their problems. Most of the time that was all right with Mack. Sometimes it was tough.

One day Mack came home and instead of calling a friend or going out to shoot baskets he slipped his headphones on, put a tape in his machine, and lay down on the couch.

When his dad came home, Mack said, "Dad, there's something going on that's really making me angry and I can't figure out what to do about it."

His dad said, "Mack, you know I'm always here to listen. What's the problem?"

Mack said, "Well, Dad, I've got this friend. He's a

real good guy and I know he's smart but he's doing
something really stupid and I can't seem to do
anything about it. The problem is that he's making
other kids do stupid things, too, and that's what really
bugs me."

"There's something you're not telling me, Mack. I
think you'd better tell me the whole story."

"O.K., Dad. It's drugs. This guy has started to
bring a lot of drugs to school and he's passing
them out to the little kids. I get so mad at him but he
just won't listen to me. He keeps saying how cool it
is and I think he really likes having the little kids think
he's something special."

"Mack, this is a problem that you can't solve by

yourself. I'm glad the problem made you angry enough to want to talk about it, because we need to do something right away."

"I know, Dad. I mean, I don't like having to turn somebody in, but when I realized he was giving it to the kids . . . yeah, I'm angry enough to do something about it."

Mack and his dad called the school principal and went to talk to her that night. The principal said she would get in touch with the boy's parents.

Driving home, Mack said, "Dad, I feel a whole lot better. I'm still angry, but at least I did something about it, right?"

"Mack," said his dad, "you did just the right thing. You're one heck of a kid. You make me proud! And don't worry about still feeling angry. That's a good kind of angry, believe me."

Mack was in a tough spot. What would you have done?

NINA'S STORY

Nina's mom sent her to the bakery one Sunday morning to get some rolls and pastry for breakfast. Nina was ten years old and liked running errands for her mom. The bakery was very busy when Nina got there, so she patiently waited her turn.

After the woman ahead of her was served, the baker waited on a woman who had come in after Nina. Nina didn't say anything, even though it made her angry. Then the man waited on someone else

who had come in after Nina. Nina got so angry that she walked out of the bakery and went home.

She told her mom what had happened. Her mom said, "Nina, why didn't you speak up when it was your turn and the baker waited on someone else?"

Nina said, "I guess I was afraid to. I was angry, but I didn't know what to do."

"I'm sure the baker didn't skip you on purpose. He probably thought that you were there with one of the adults. Why don't you go back and try again, and tell the baker what happened the first time."

Nina went back to the bakery. It was less crowded, and she didn't have to wait for long. When it was

her turn, she said to the baker, "When I was here before, you ignored me, and that wasn't right."

The man said, "I did? Oh, I'm so sorry. It gets so busy here on Sundays that sometimes I don't know what I'm doing. I am sorry. What can I get for you now?"

Nina bought the rolls and pastry and headed home. She felt a lot better. She was glad that she had spoken up and made her feelings known.

What would you do?

TOMMY'S STORY

Tommy was seven and he loved collecting baseball cards. He had more players than any of the kids he knew. He worked hard to make the money he needed to buy new cards. He did chores in the neighborhood, raking lawns, taking out garbage, and sweeping sidewalks.

One day, his dad saw him moping around and looking kind of irritated. Tommy would take some

coins out of his pocket, look at them and frown, and put the money away. He did this again and again, until his dad asked him what was wrong.

Tommy said, "Aw, nothing, Dad." But from the way he said it, his dad could tell something was wrong.

"You can't fool me, Tommy," his dad said. "Come on, tell me what's wrong."

"Oh, it's my own fault, Dad," Tommy said. "Mr. Miller down at the store cheated me out of twenty-five cents when I bought some baseball cards today. I didn't realize it until after I got home."

"Well," his dad said, "why don't you go back to the store and tell Mr. Miller he didn't give you the right change. I'm sure it was just a mistake. That's better than sitting there feeling angry about it."

"No, I can't do that, Dad," Tommy said. "It's too late now."

His dad said, "Tommy, if someone does something that makes you angry, you have to speak up and tell them how you feel. Otherwise, you're going to feel cheated and angry and unhappy. Give it a try."

Tommy did. He went to Mr. Miller's store and told him what happened. Mr. Miller said, "Oh, I'm sorry, Tommy. Here's a quarter. You've always been honest with me, and if you say I owe you a quarter, then I owe you a quarter."

Tommy felt better immediately, and he realized that he should have spoken up sooner. Then he wouldn't have felt angry with Mr. Miller for what was just a simple mistake.

What would you do if you were Tommy?

SOPHIE'S STORY

Sophie was nine years old. She had long blond hair, big brown eyes, and peaches-and-cream skin. Sophie was also smart and popular. One day what Sophie was most of all was angry.

She came home, ran up to her room, slammed the door, put the music on, and just kicked. Sophie kicked her bed, she kicked her desk, and then she kicked the chair and broke it.

"Sophie!" said her mom, opening the door. "For heaven's sake, what's wrong! I've never seen you so wild and angry! You must tell me what the problem is."

"Oh, Mom," said Sophie. "Everything's wrong and it's not my fault. I'm just so angry at Becky I feel like punching her."

"But, Sophie, Becky's your best friend. What happened?"

"Mom, Becky got angry because I got picked as team captain for soccer. She told me she hated me and she said she wasn't going to be my friend anymore. But that's not the worst part. This afternoon she told Sharon, Julie, and Rennie that I had been talking about them behind their backs. She told them I'd said nasty things about them and I didn't!"

"How do you know she told the girls that, Sophie?" asked her mom.

"Rennie came up to me after school and started yelling at me. I asked her what it was all about and that's how I found out about Becky. Oh, Mom. How could she turn around and be such a creep? We were best friends! I didn't want to go out for team

captain. That was Becky's idea. She said it would be fun to see who won—me or her."

"Well, Sophie," said her mom, "it sounds like you and Becky have some talking to do."

"Talking!" said Sophie. "I never want to talk to her again!"

"Sophie, that's just your anger speaking. If you take a minute to think, maybe you'll realize that Becky was just feeling bad about losing. She went overboard and acted foolishly out of anger, just as you are now. You don't really want to lose a friend over something dumb like this, do you?" asked Sophie's mom.

"I guess not," said Sophie. "Maybe I'll call her and ask if we can talk about it."

"Good girl, Sophie," said her mom. "That's a very mature thing to do and I'm proud of you. I hope that you and Becky will work things out."

What would you do if you were Sophie?

JAY'S STORY

Music was just about the most important thing in Jay's life. He loved any kind of music—rock, country, classical, jazz, anything. Jay was ten and had been taking piano lessons for three years.

Jay had just gotten a new piano teacher, Mr. Benson. Jay liked Mr. Benson in many ways. He was a good teacher. But there was one thing about Mr. Benson that Jay didn't like, and it made him angry.

Mr. Benson had a habit of rapping Jay on the knuckles with a pointer when he made a mistake.

Jay didn't say anything to Mr. Benson about it, but one day he told his dad how angry the knuckle-rapping made him. His dad said, "Have you told Mr. Benson how you feel about it?"

Jay said no, he hadn't.

His dad said, "Well, Jay, why don't you tell him that it makes you angry? If you feel that way when he does it, and you keep those feelings inside, it's going to affect you during the lessons. When you're angry about something, it's very hard to concentrate on the things you should be doing."

Jay said, "Whatever I say, I don't think it will make him stop, Dad."

His dad said, "Jay, please take my advice and speak up."

Jay did. He told Mr. Benson exactly how he felt, and he said that his anger was distracting him from his piano playing.

Mr. Benson apologized. He said, "You're absolutely right, Jay. That's a very bad habit I have. You know, when I was learning how to play piano, my teacher used to smack my knuckles. Then when I became a teacher, I guess I remembered and started doing it myself. I'll tell you what. If I slip up and do it again, you have my permission to rap my knuckles. Maybe that'll help me remember not to do it anymore!"

Mr. Benson and Jay both laughed and got back to their music.

What would you do?

SUSAN'S STORY

Susan's mom met her at the front door when she got home from school one day. Susan was eight and in the second grade.

Her mom said, "Susan, your teacher called and told me something about your behavior at school today. If it's true, I'm very disappointed with you. Your teacher said you got very angry with Jeannie Curtis and called her some very mean names. And she said it isn't the first time you've done this. Is that true?"

Susan said, "I'm sorry, Mom. I didn't mean to say

those things. Jeannie took some loose-leaf paper from my desk without asking me. I got very angry about it. I'm really sorry."

Her mom said, "Susan, I can understand your getting angry, but it isn't right to say insulting things about anyone. Being angry is O.K. Being mean out of anger is not O.K."

"I know that, Mom," Susan said. "I guess I can't control myself when I get angry."

Her mom said, "I know you feel bad about it now. There are things you can do to help yourself from behaving that way out of anger."

"Like what, Mom?" Susan asked.

"Well, one thing you can do," her mom said, is to think about your anger every time you start to feel that way. Say to yourself, 'I'm getting angry.' Then

think, 'Why am I getting angry, and how am I going to behave?' If you're angry with someone, tell her how you feel. But that's all. Just let her know what your feelings are. That's the important thing."

"I'll try, Mom," Susan said. "I'll really try. And tomorrow I'll apologize to Jeannie for being so mean. It isn't worth hurting someone's feelings over a few sheets of paper."

What can you do to control your temper and watch your words?

CHRIS'S STORY

Chris was ten when his mom decided to go back to work. The whole family had talked about it and decided that if Mom really wanted to do it, it was O.K. by them.

Since his mom wasn't around during the day anymore, Chris and his older brother, Jack, and younger sister, Sue, shared many of the responsibilities of the house. One day Chris came home very angry and broke three dishes while he was putting them away.

Jack was in the kitchen fixing himself a snack. He said, "What's wrong, Chris? You look like you're really angry about something. Want to talk about it?"

"Oh, some of the guys went to the field to practice

batting after school today. I just wish I could've gone with them," Chris said.

"Gee, Chris, why didn't you go? You could've stayed for a while and then come home to do your chores."

"It wouldn't have been the same, knowing I had to leave in the middle of it," Chris said. "And I probably would've gotten in trouble anyway. I mean, I've got jobs to do around here and I'm the one that has to do them, right?"

"That's true, Chris," said Jack. "But you've got to spend time with your friends, too. Listen, instead of being angry, why don't you just try to figure out how to do both—spend time with your friends and get your jobs around the house done."

"I don't know, Jack. I feel like Mom's counting on me to do my part around here and I don't want to let her down," Chris said.

"I've got an idea, Chris. Why don't you trade jobs with me? I'll put the dishes away in the afternoon if you load the washer after dinner. That way you can

play with your buddies after school and I'll have more time to do my homework at night."

"That's a great idea, Jack," Chris said. "You're sure you wouldn't mind?"

"Of course not, Chris," said Jack. "That's what brothers are for. But one thing you've got to remember, Chris. When you're feeling angry about something, it always helps to talk about it. Sometimes we can't find the answers ourselves. That's what brothers and families are really for, O.K.?"

"O.K., Jack. Thanks."

What would you do if you were Chris?

MARGARET'S STORY

Margaret was eight and her best friends were Priscilla and Judy. The three of them went everywhere together. They were in the same class at school and in the same clubs at church.

Margaret came home from school very angry. She

told her mom, "I'm not friends with Priscilla and Judy anymore. I'll never talk to them again!"

Her mom was very surprised. "Margaret," she said, "what would ever make you say that?"

"This weekend they went to see the movie we were planning to see together," Margaret said. "They didn't tell me they were going or ask me to come along and I'm really angry about it."

Her mom said, "Did you tell Priscilla and Judy how you feel? Maybe there was a mix-up or a misunderstanding."

The next day at school, Margaret saw Priscilla and Judy in the hall. At first, she wasn't going to say

anything about how angry she was. Finally, she
spoke up and told the girls how upset she was that
they had gone to the movie without her.

Priscilla and Judy were very surprised. They had
thought that Margaret and her family had gone
away for the weekend. So of course they didn't ask
her to go to the movie with them. Margaret felt a lot
better now that she knew it was just a misunderstanding.
After all, Priscilla and Judy were her best friends in
the world, and it didn't make sense to lose two
friendships over a simple misunderstanding.

Suppose that a friend of yours left you out of his or
her plans *on purpose*. How do you think you'd
feel? What would you do?

ERNEST'S STORY

Ernest was five and had a hard time controlling his temper. When things didn't go right for him, he would get very angry, and then he would throw something or break something. Sometimes he would hit one of his friends.

His mom told him, "Ernest, it's O.K. to get angry, but when you do, it's not O.K. to hurt anyone or damage anything."

Ernest would say, "I'm sorry, Mom. I just couldn't help it."

One day Ernest got angry when he was playing with his best friend, Billy. He hit Billy, and Billy got very upset. "I'm not going to play with you anymore," he told Ernest. Then Billy went home.

Ernest felt very bad about what had happened. He told his mom about it. "I didn't really want to hurt Billy," he said. "Now he won't play with me. What can I do, Mom?"

His mom said, "Ernest, do you really want to do something about the way you behave when you get angry?"

Ernest said, "Yes, Mom."

"Well," his mom said, "there are a lot of things you can do. Let's try one, and if that doesn't work, we'll try something else."

"All right, Mom," Ernest said.

His mom said, "The next time you start feeling angry about something, Ernest, stick your hands in your pockets. Think hard about keeping your hands in your pockets. If someone does something to make you angry, tell that person how you feel. But concentrate on keeping your hands in your pockets."

Ernest tried it. It was a real struggle, and sometimes he still broke things or hit people, but not often. It got easier to keep his hands in his pockets, and Ernest felt a lot better about the way he behaved when he got angry.

Would Ernest's trick work for you? What else could you do instead of being destructive?

HILLARY'S STORY

Hillary was eight and in the second grade. She was a pretty good student. She worked very hard and did her homework every night.

One day the teacher gave the class a test. Hillary had studied hard and was ready for the test. While she was taking the test, Hillary glanced around and saw that Paula, who sat next to her, was copying her answers. Hillary couldn't say anything because the teacher didn't allow talking during the test, and when the test was over, it was time to go home.

That evening when Hillary's mom got home, Hillary told her what had happened. Hillary said, "I don't know what to do about it, Mom, but it makes me mad."

Her mom said, "Why didn't you tell the teacher after class? That would have been the right thing to do and it would have made you feel better."

Hillary said, "Gee, Mom, I wanted to, but everyone was getting ready to leave and Paula was watching me. All of the kids like Paula. If I said something, she'd know I told on her and then no one would like me."

Her mom said, "Well, Hillary, if you don't speak up, Paula may think her copying is O.K. with you. Then she might never stop. I'm sure the other kids won't care. In fact, they'll probably admire you for standing up for yourself."

Hillary said, "But what should I do, Mom?"

Her mom said, "First, you should tell your teacher

what happened. Then you should tell Paula how
you feel. Why don't you practice with me? What
would you say to me if I were Paula?"

Hillary thought very hard, then said, "I'd tell Paula,
'I'm angry at you for copying from me on the test. I
don't want you to do it again. It's cheating and it's
wrong.'"

The next day, Hillary felt very brave when she
talked to her teacher before class. The teacher said
she would talk to Paula. And when Paula sat down
next to Hillary, Hillary told her exactly what she felt,
just the way she'd practiced it with her mom. Paula
didn't say much, but Hillary knew she understood,
and Hillary felt much better.

If someone copied from your test, what would you
do?